discovermore

Exploring Life Science

Habitats and Biomes

Ernest Brazzos

Britannica Educational Publishing

IN ASSOCIATION WITH

THE ROSEN PUBLISHING GROUP

Published in 2025 by The Rosen Publishing Group, Inc.
2544 Clinton Street, Buffalo, NY 14224

Editor: Brianna Propis
Book Design: Michael Flynn

Photo Credits: Cover Kuznetsov Alexey/Shutterstock.com; (series background) Dai Yim/Shutterstock.com; p. 5 Irina Markova/Shutterstock.com; p. 6 Jess Lang/Shutterstock.com; p. 7 Vladimir Melnikov/Shutterstock.com; p. 8 Ethan Daniels/Shutterstock.com; p. 9 koliw/Shutterstock.com; p. 10 Ruslan Suseynov/Shutterstock.com; p. 11 olena2552/Shutterstock.com; p. 12 Dennis W Donohue/Shutterstock.com; p. 13 HelloRF Zcool/Shutterstock.com; p. 14 Maxim Weise/Shutterstock.com; p. 15 syachin/Shutterstock.com; p. 17 (top) Richard G Smith/Shutterstock.com; p. 17 (bottom) Scott E Read/Shutterstock.com; p. 18 worldclassphoto/Shutterstock.com; p. 19 Tarcisio Schnaider/Shutterstock.com; p. 20 Irina Shatilova/Shutterstock.com; p. 21 Vaclav Sebek/Shutterstock.com; p. 23 I T A L O/Shutterstock.com; p. 24 melissamn/Shutterstock.com; p. 25 Dennis W Donohue/Shutterstock.com; p. 26 Vladimir Endovitskiy/Shutterstock.com; p. 27 Alexey Seafarer/Shutterstock.com; p. 29 Tatiana Grozetskaya/Shutterstock.com.

Library of Congress Cataloging-in-Publication Data

Names: Brazzos, Ernest, author.
Title: Habitats and biomes / Ernest Brazzos.
Description: [Buffalo] : Britannica Educational Publishing, [2025] | Series: Discover more! Exploring life science | Includes bibliographical references and index.
Identifiers: LCCN 2023051662 (print) | LCCN 2023051663 (ebook) | ISBN 9781641901628 (library binding) | ISBN 9781641901611 (paperback) | ISBN 9781641901635 (ebook)
Subjects: LCSH: Habitat (Ecology)--Juvenile literature | Biotic communities--Juvenile literature | Ecology--Juvenile literature.
Classification: LCC QH541.14 .B73344 2025 (print) | LCC QH541.14 (ebook) | DDC 577--dc23/eng/20231222
LC record available at https://lccn.loc.gov/2023051662
LC ebook record available at https://lccn.loc.gov/2023051663

Manufactured in the United States of America

Some of the images in this book illustrate individuals who are models. The depictions do not imply actual situations or events.

CPSIA Compliance Information: Batch #CSBRIT25. For further information contact Rosen Publishing at 1-800-237-9932.

Contents

What Are Habitats and Biomes?

A habitat is the natural home or environment of animals, plants, and other organisms. Habitats provide living things with everything they need to survive, such as water, shelter, and food.

Habitats can be very small **microhabitats**, such as a leaf, or large, such as a forest. Biomes are typically larger than habitats.

A biome is a large area with specific types of climate and animal species. Climate is the usual pattern of weather found in a place. For example, deserts have a hot, dry climate. Biomes include oceans, rainforests, grasslands, and deserts. Each biome can include many different habitats with a variety of animal species.

compare and contrast

How are habitats and biomes similar?
How do they differ from each other?

The largest biome in the world is the water biome. It includes the five major oceans that cover 70 percent of Earth.

WORD WISE

A TINY HABITAT IS CALLED A MICROHABITAT. FOR EXAMPLE, SMALL ORGANISMS MIGHT LIVE IN A TEMPORARY POOL OF WATER OR UNDERNEATH A ROCK.

Survival Skills

Every habitat and biome has a unique set of conditions, such as how hot or cold it is, whether it's wet or dry, and whether the ground is made up of soil, sand, or rock. The plants and animals living in a habitat have developed survival skills that help them live there. These skills are called **adaptations**.

During cold winters, wood frogs freeze 60 percent of their bodies solid. Their bodies adapted to produce a special compound that makes them able to stop breathing and stop their hearts from beating.

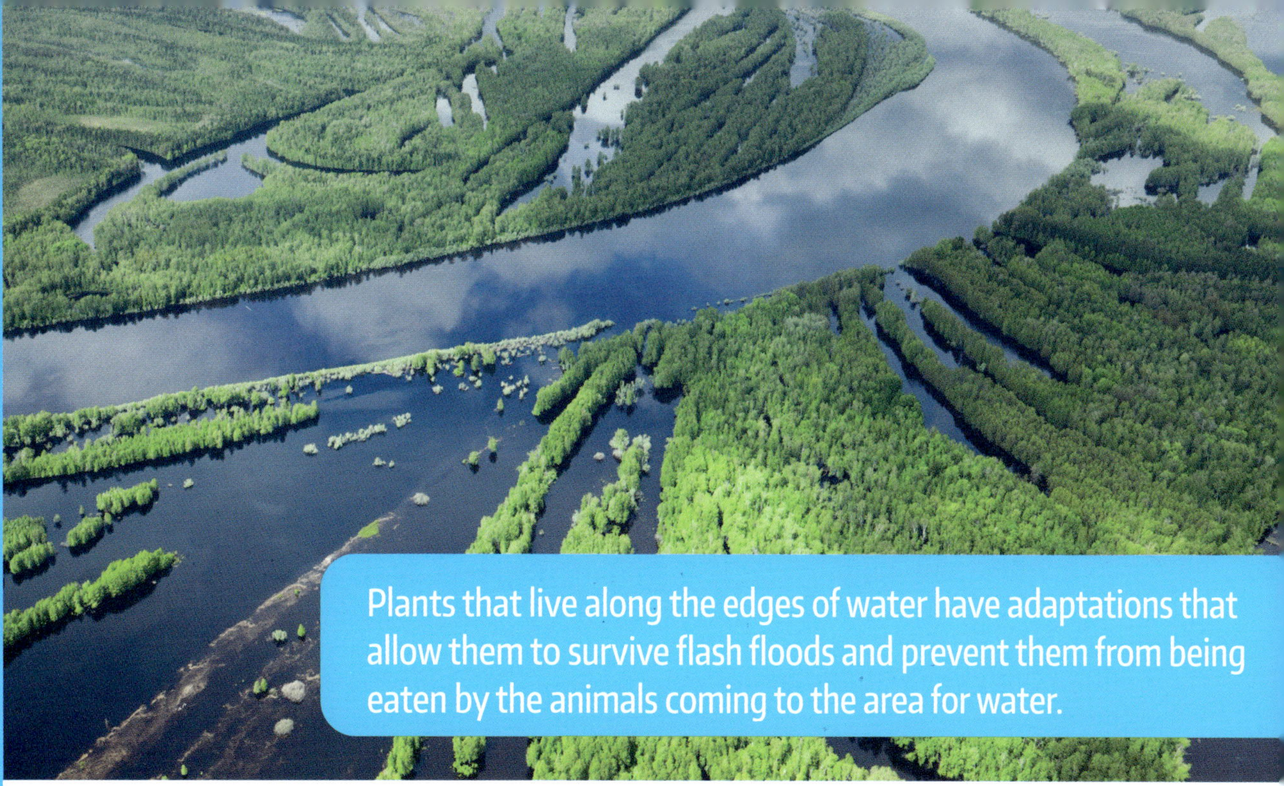

Some plants have adapted to withstand the cold and windy conditions of a mountain. Others have adaptations to help them live in ponds and lakes. Most birds have wings to fly, but a penguin's wings are adapted for swimming. Most living things have adaptations that help them survive in one or two types of habitats, but they would not be suited for survival in other habitats.

WORD WISE

ADAPTATIONS ARE SPECIAL FEATURES THAT HELP AN ANIMAL SURVIVE IN ITS HABITAT. THIS INCREASES THE ANIMAL'S ABILITY TO REPRODUCE.

Salty Biomes

Of all the water on Earth's surface, 96.5 percent of it is salt water. This area is home to many organisms. Few plants live in deep seas. Near the coast, there are plantlike seaweeds. Seawater is salty and salt kills most plants, but seaweed leaves have a thick coating that protects them from the salt. Seaweeds need light to make food, so some of them have leaves that float to the surface to reach the light for photosynthesis.

Algae have adapted to exist in underwater habitats that receive little or no sunlight.

Aquatic animals, such as fish, have gills to help them breathe underwater.

Ocean animals have adapted to live at sea and breathe underwater. Aquatic animals that can't breathe underwater, such as dolphins, come to the surface to breathe air. In deep, dark water, dolphins use **echolocation** to find food. They make clicking noises and then figure out where fish are from the echoes.

WORD WISE

ECHOLOCATION IS AN ADAPTATION ANIMALS USE TO FIGURE OUT WHERE THINGS, SUCH AS PREY, ARE BY BOUNCING ECHOES OFF THEM. DOLPHINS USE THIS UNDERWATER, AND BATS USE THIS ON LAND.

Freshwater Biomes

Freshwater biomes, such as rivers, ponds, and lakes, contain water that isn't salty. Like all plants, those that grow in freshwater must reach the light. Plants such as sedges, a grass-like species, and irises, a type of flower, grow by the water's edge. They have stiff stems to hold up their leaves. Lilies have long stems that enable their leaves to reach the water's surface.

A water lily has flat, rounded leaves that float like rafts. They have air-filled spaces that prevent them from sinking.

Cattails have air-filled tubes that carry oxygen down to the base of the plant.

Some animals, such as fish, live underwater their whole lives—without needing to come up for air. Fish swim by moving their tails and fins. They eat underwater plants and other animals.

Other animals live by water and visit it to feed. Otters have webbed feet to help them swim to find food. Ducks may dive underwater to catch their food, such as fish or aquatic plants.

Consider This

River water can move quickly, while pond water tends to be more still. How could this affect the way leaves grow inside these bodies of water?

Soggy Biomes

Wetlands, such as swamps and marshes, are underwater for most of the year.

Plants that grow in wetlands have many roots to anchor themselves in the soggy ground. Rice can only grow if its roots are in marshy ground. Due to this, farmers build walls to hold water in rice fields. They also use clay soil.

Swamps are home to many wildlife species, such as alligators, shrimps, and frogs.

Wetlands help fight climate change! Older freshwater wetlands remove more carbon from the atmosphere than they release into it.

Although "wet" is in their name, sometimes wetlands dry up. Mudskippers, a kind of amphibious fish, have developed special features to cope with this. Like all other fishes, they have gills so they can breathe underwater. However, when the water dries up, their gills can carry a supply of air. They are able to then breathe on land.

Consider This

Many animals use camouflage, or the ability to blend in with their surroundings, to survive. How might a wetland animal use camouflage to stay alive?

Woody Biomes

Some biomes are full of trees. These are known as woodlands. Woodlands grow in places with warm, rainy springs and summers, and cold, dry falls and winters. The maple, oak, and beech trees that grow in woodlands are **deciduous**. That means they change with the seasons. In fall, they lose their leaves. This stops the cold from damaging them. The trees do not grow new leaves until the spring.

The leaves of deciduous trees change color before falling off. They usually become yellow, red, or orange!

Woodpeckers break holes in tree bark by pecking on it to find and eat beetles. They prefer dead trees.

Woodland trees are sources of food and shelter for a variety of creatures. Worms and beetles eat rotting leaves on the woodland floor. Badgers dig homes between the tree roots. They come out at night to eat worms and slugs. Mice nibble seeds and berries that fall from trees. Birds make their nests in the trees and feed on insects and fruit that are found in the bark and branches.

WORD WISE

DECIDUOUS MEANS "TO FALL OFF." EVERY FALL, DECIDUOUS TREES LOSE THEIR LEAVES.

Green Leaves

Most trees have green leaves, but only some have them year-round! These are called conifer trees. Forests of conifer trees grow in places with long, cold winters. Conifer trees have dark green leaves that are long and thin, like needles. Pine, spruce, and fir are conifer trees. Because they keep their leaves throughout the entire year, they're also called evergreen.

Certain animals live in conifer forests. Pine sawflies lay their eggs inside pine needles. The young that hatch eat the leaves. Ants make nests from piles of old pine needles. Mammals, such as the lynx, develop a thick fur coat to keep it warm while on the prowl, or hunt, for food.

compare and contrast

Would a bird that makes a nest in a deciduous tree have a different experience than one nesting in a conifer tree? Why or why not?

Bristlecone pines are the oldest living trees in the world. Some of them are over 4,000 years old.

Some grizzly bears live in coniferous forests. They feed on insects, berries, nuts, and fish.

Always Rainy

Plants and trees in rainforests grow where it rains almost every day—hence the name. These are ideal conditions for plants to grow, so trees here can be very tall. Rainforests can support more kinds of life than any other habitat because of their frequent moisture and sunlight.

The largest rainforest in the world is the Amazon in South America. More than 40,000 plants and over 4,000 animal species live there.

The trees that grow Brazil nuts are known as Brazil nut trees (*Bertholletia excelsa*). They can grow to 160 feet (49 m) or more!

The animals that live in the rainforest can flourish because of its features. Tree frogs drink from pools of rainwater that collect in giant leaves. Monkeys have long arms and fingers. These help the animals grip branches, so they can move easily through the trees to find fruit to eat. Birds, such as the colorful toucan, have big, hard beaks. These beaks help them to crack open and eat rainforest nuts known as Brazil nuts.

Consider This

What conditions does a rainforest have to support a large number of animals and plants that other biomes might not have?

No Rain

While it's not uncommon for a desert to be a sandy, hot, and dry place, there are other kinds of deserts as well. A desert is any large region that gets very little rain each year. These are difficult habitats for plants to live in. Cactus plants have thick stems that store water when it does rain. Desert grasses have very long roots. They spread out below the surface to help the grass absorb the small amount of water that's available.

Cactus stems have a layer of protection to help prevent evaporation. They also have spikes to stop desert animals from drinking the water inside them.

Gila monsters, a type of large lizard, live most of their lives underground in burrows, or holes. They only come above ground at night or if it's cooler during the day.

Many animals that live in the desert don't drink water directly. Instead, they get the water they need from plants or plant seeds that hold a lot of water. Gerbils eat seeds, and they live under rocks or burrow under sand. Baird's pocket gophers cleverly camouflage their burrows, as mounds of dirt are the only visible part of their underground shelters.

Consider This

Why do you think most desert animals are nocturnal, or only active at night?

Grassy Biomes

Many types of plants struggle to grow in grasslands because the weather is too dry, and the soil isn't rich. The land is covered mainly in grasses. **Tropical grasslands** grow close to the equator. Temperate grasslands grow in regions farther from the equator.

Grasses are tough plants. Their roots lie just below the surface so they can catch any rain that falls. Their leaves grow back very quickly if animals eat them. Grasslands located in North America are usually called prairies.

Unsurprisingly, plenty of grassland animals feed on grass! Prairie dogs eat grass and then scurry into underground holes to escape eagles. Grazing animals, such as zebras and antelope, live in groups called herds. Lions and cheetahs hunt and kill grazing animals for food.

Consider This

Some animals, such as prairie dogs, often travel in groups. How could this help them to defend themselves from predators more easily?

Grassland prairie dogs protect themselves from predators with their fast speed, sharp claws, and powerful teeth.

WORD WISE

TROPICAL GRASSLANDS ARE OFTEN CALLED SAVANNAS.

Tough Leaves

Plants in scrublands have tough, leathery leaves that hold a lot of water. Scrublands are hot and dry in summer but cool and wet in winter. Small trees and bushy plants with woody stems, such as rosemary and lavender, grow here. Some plants also have thorns or strong-smelling oils to stop animals from eating them.

Some scrublands are the result of land being affected by a major fire.

Some moose live in scrublands. Their large, two-toed hooves give them better balance as they walk on the ground.

Scrubland places offer seeds and berries for animals, such as brush rabbits, to find and eat. The animals hide in the low-growing plants as they look for food. Jackrabbits eat mostly grasses. They have furry feet to protect them from the hot ground. Moose are herbivores, meaning they only eat plants. They feed on the leaves and twigs of woody trees and plants, as well as grasses and shrubs.

Consider This

Many of the trees in scrublands are short. What conditions could prevent tall trees from growing in scrublands?

Frozen Biomes

The tundra is the coldest of all biomes. It is land near the Arctic that is covered in ice and snow during winter. Tundra biomes are warmer during the short summers, but even then, the soil stays frozen. Some plants grow quickly in summer and die during winter. Most plants grow low to the ground to avoid the harsh, cold wind. Many animals visit the tundra in the summer to eat the plants but leave the area before winter.

Many plants in the tundra have small, waxy leaves and hairy stems that help them hold moisture.

Certain tundra animals, such as Arctic foxes, use camouflage by turning white in the winter.

Some animals can survive in the tundra all year long. Polar bears dive into icy Arctic seas to catch seals. They have thick fur and a layer of blubber to keep them warm. Birds that live in the tundra usually have two layers of thick feathers to keep them warm.

Consider This

When humans are cold, they might put a jacket on or stay inside their homes. What are some ways animals in the tundra keep warm?

People as Predators

The largest predators to habitats and biomes—and the living things within them—are people. For example, people drain wetlands and dig up grasslands to make space for towns, factories, and airports. Pollution damages habitats too. Rivers become polluted when factory waste or oil runs into them. The animals lose their homes and are left with nowhere to go and no food to feed themselves or their babies.

There are a variety of ways people can protect the habitats and biomes of wildlife and plants. They make laws to stop pollution. They plant new trees. In some places, people develop **nature preserves** or national parks.

Consider This

What could happen if animals and plants continue to lose their habitats and biomes? How does a loss of habitat affect the wildlife that lives there?

Rising temperatures from global warming harm the balance between animals, plants, and their ecosystems. Plants adapt by blooming earlier or growing in cooler locations, and the species that rely on them for food are forced to change environments.

WORD WISE

NATURE PRESERVES ARE PROTECTED AREAS OF LAND WHERE IT'S ILLEGAL FOR ANYONE TO CHANGE OR HARM THE WILDLIFE AND PLANTS LIVING THERE.

Glossary

aquatic Growing, living, or often found in water.

blubber A thick layer of fat.

conifer A tree with needlelike leaves. Conifers have leaves all year round.

echolocation Locating objects, such as prey, by sound and vibration.

ecosystem A group of living things that live with other living things in an environment.

evaporation The process of a liquid turning into vapor.

graze Feeding on growing grass or herbs.

photosynthesis The process of green plants turning sunlight into food.

species A group of similar living organisms that reproduce.

temperate A grassland that has plants with long roots that dig deep into the soil.

temporary Something that lasts only a short time.

tropical A place with temperatures that are warm or hot throughout the year.

webbed Having skin that stretches between fingers and toes.

For More Information

Books

Andrews, Elizabeth. *Forest Biomes*. Minneapolis, MN: Cody Koala, 2022.

Latham, Donna, and Tom Casteel. *Biomes: Discover the Earth's Ecosystems with Environmental Science Activities for Kids*. White River Junction, VT: Nomad Press, 2019.

Woodward, John, and Nick Crumpton. *Habitats of the World: A Breathtaking Visual Journey Through Earth's Incredible Ecosystems*. New York, NY: DK Publishing, 2023.

Websites

National Geographic: Biomes
education.nationalgeographic.org/resource/resource-library-biomes/
Learn about the biomes around the world and the many creatures within them.

National Geographic: Habitats
kids.nationalgeographic.com/nature/habitats
Learn about the different natural environments of animals and plants.

Wilderness Classroom
wildernessclassroom.org/understanding-habitats-ecosystems-biomes/
Explore habitats, ecosystems, and biomes with informative articles and worksheets.

Index